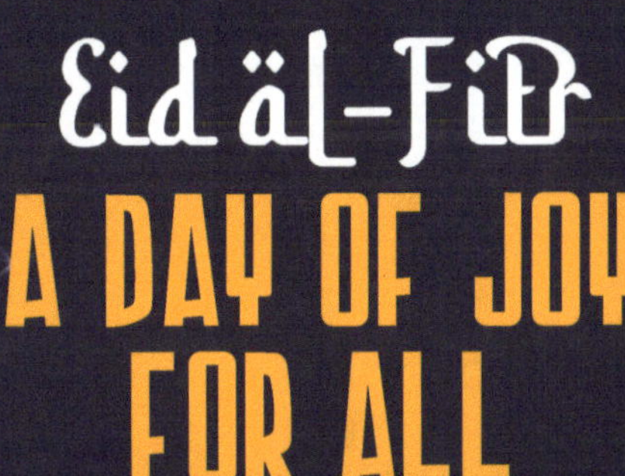

Eid al-Fitr
A DAY OF JOY FOR ALL

Zabed Mohammad, PhD.

Educator & Researcher
Canada

Once upon a time, in a small town in Windsor, Ontario, Canada, there lived a young boy named Alex. He was an inquisitive and curious lad, always eager to learn about new cultures and traditions, and one day, he heard about a fascinating celebration called Eid al-Fitr.

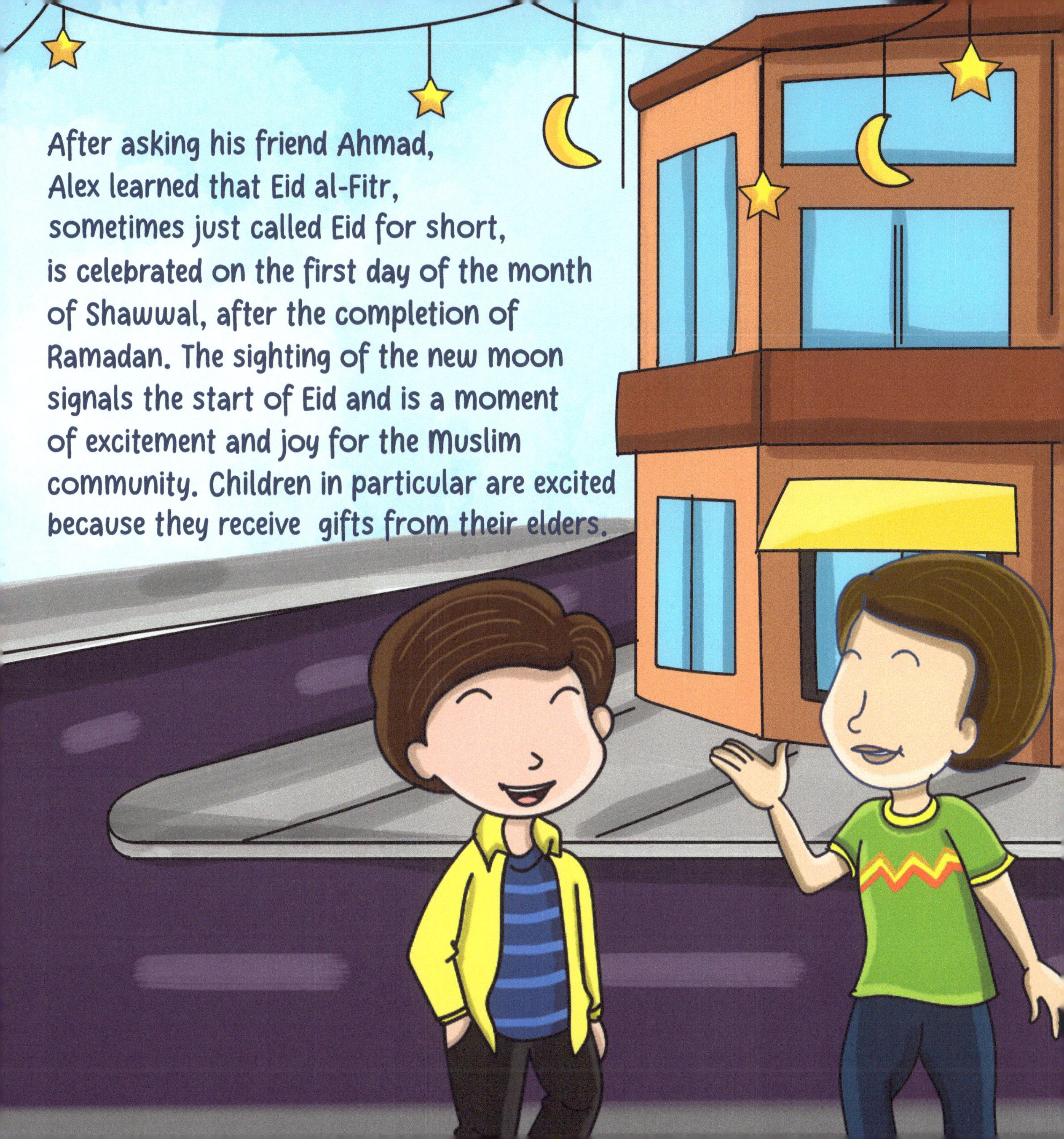

After asking his friend Ahmad, Alex learned that Eid al-Fitr, sometimes just called Eid for short, is celebrated on the first day of the month of Shawwal, after the completion of Ramadan. The sighting of the new moon signals the start of Eid and is a moment of excitement and joy for the Muslim community. Children in particular are excited because they receive gifts from their elders.

Alex was intrigued and wanted to know more, so Ahmad decided to take him to his community's Eid celebration, which was taking place the next day.

Alex observed a vibrant and festive atmosphere as he walked through the streets towards the mosque on Eid al-Fitr. The air was filled with the scent of delicious food being cooked in homes and the sound of children laughing and playing with their new toys.
EID MUBARAK

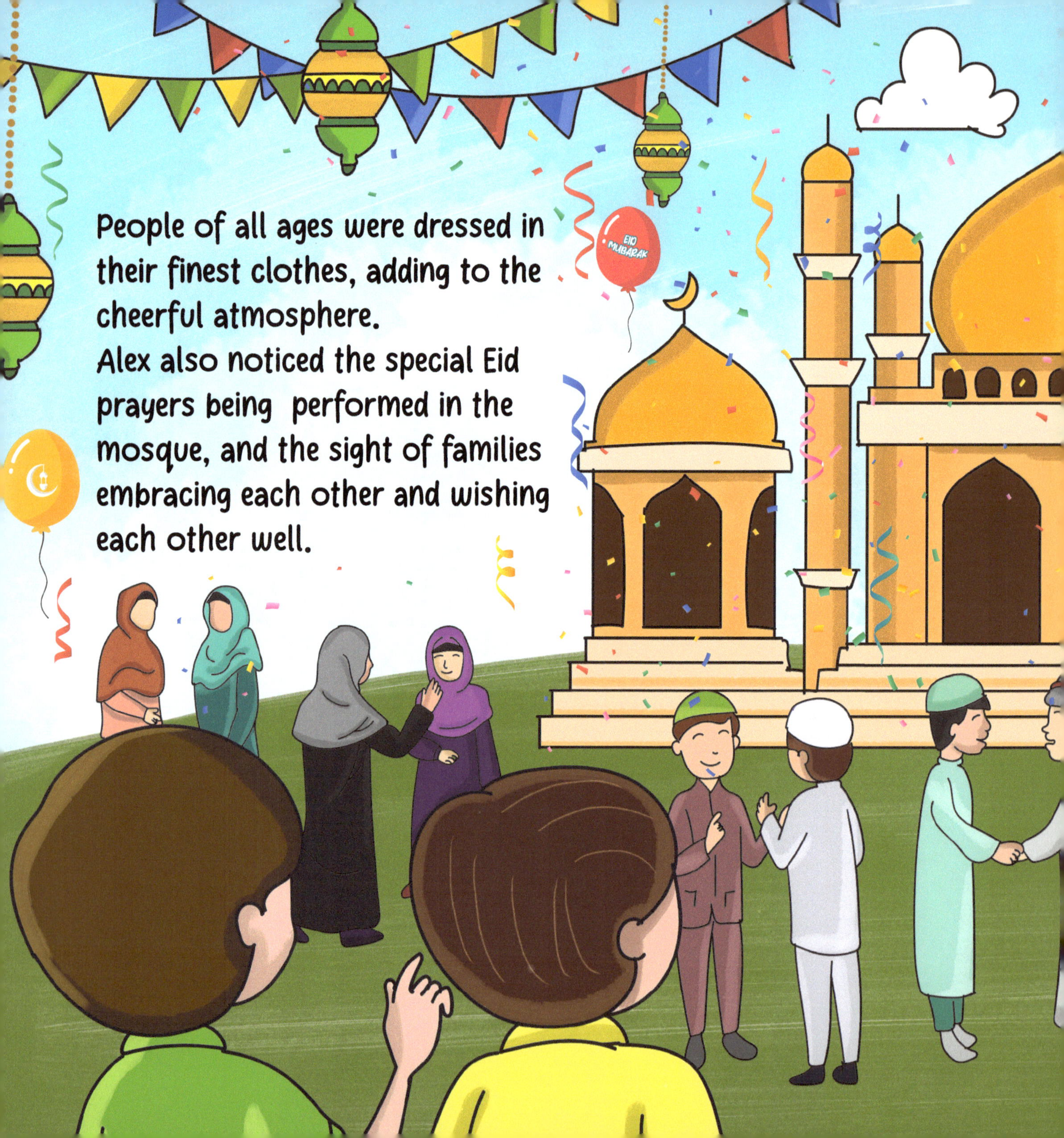

People of all ages were dressed in their finest clothes, adding to the cheerful atmosphere.
Alex also noticed the special Eid prayers being performed in the mosque, and the sight of families embracing each other and wishing each other well.

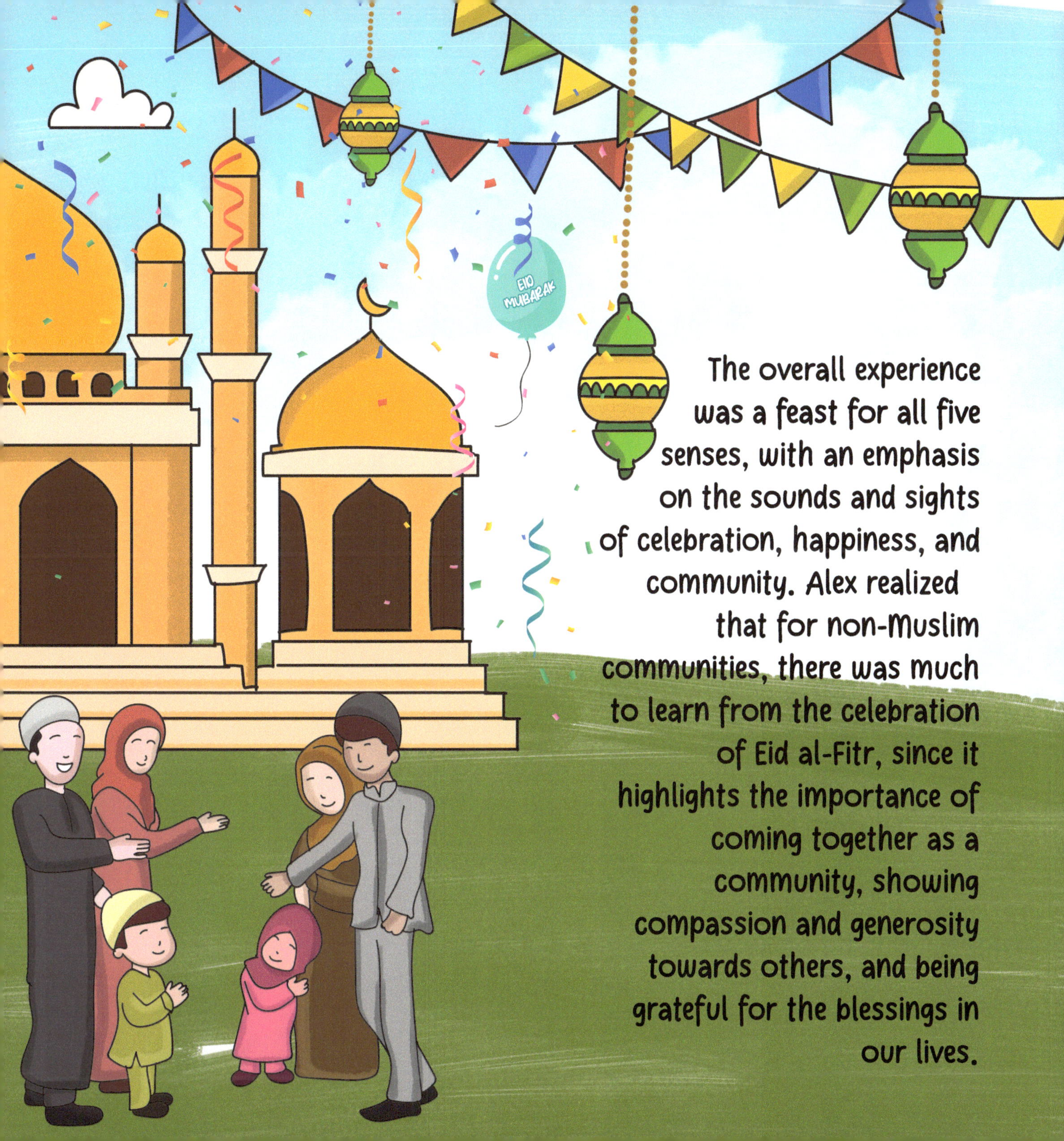

The overall experience was a feast for all five senses, with an emphasis on the sounds and sights of celebration, happiness, and community. Alex realized that for non-Muslim communities, there was much to learn from the celebration of Eid al-Fitr, since it highlights the importance of coming together as a community, showing compassion and generosity towards others, and being grateful for the blessings in our lives.

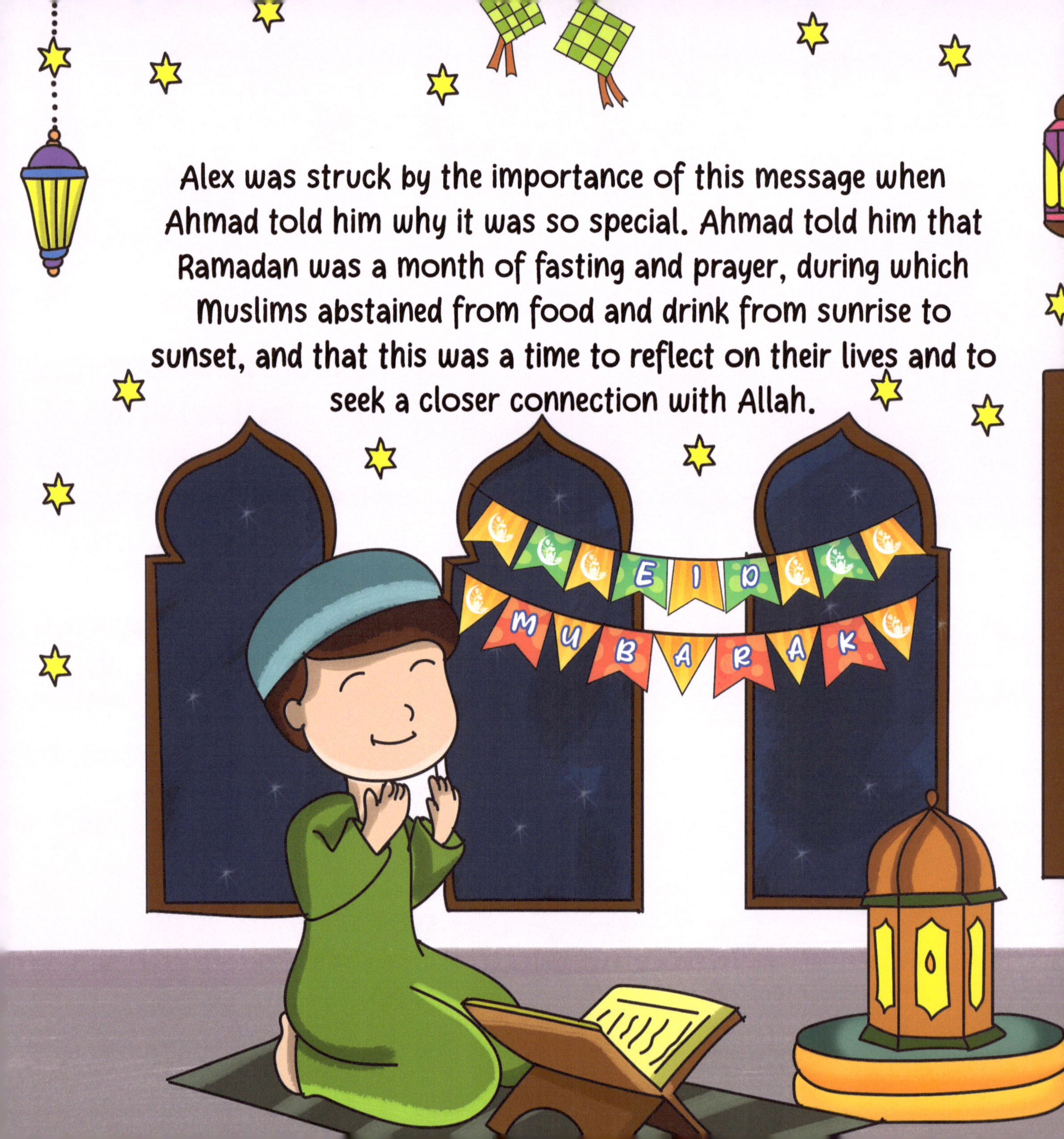

Alex was struck by the importance of this message when Ahmad told him why it was so special. Ahmad told him that Ramadan was a month of fasting and prayer, during which Muslims abstained from food and drink from sunrise to sunset, and that this was a time to reflect on their lives and to seek a closer connection with Allah.

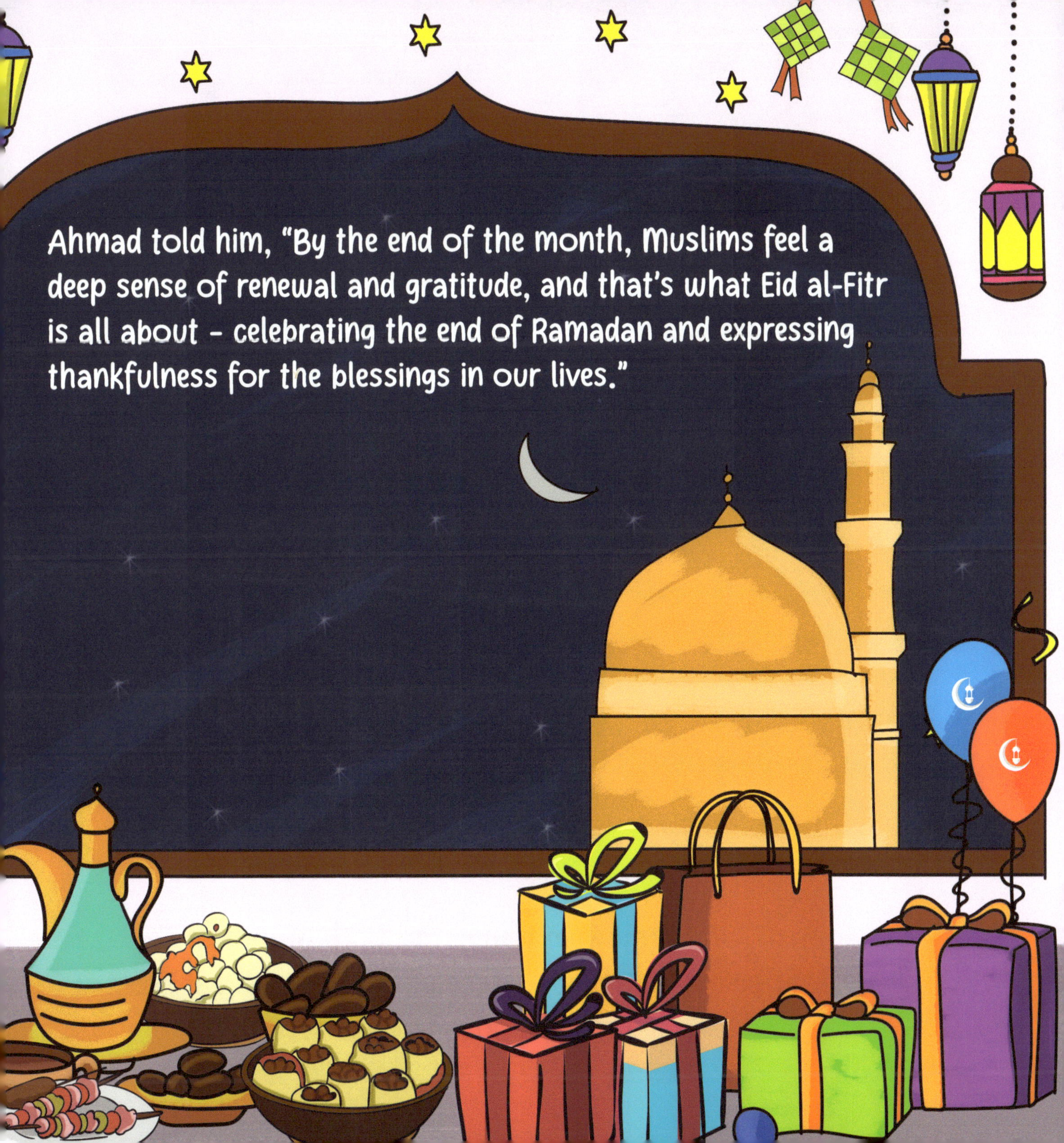

Ahmad told him, "By the end of the month, Muslims feel a deep sense of renewal and gratitude, and that's what Eid al-Fitr is all about – celebrating the end of Ramadan and expressing thankfulness for the blessings in our lives."

EID MUBARAK
Alex: Hey, Ahmad, can you tell me more about Eid al-Fitr and Ramadan?
Ahmad: Sure, Alex! Ramadan is the ninth month of the Islamic calendar, and it's a time when Muslims fast every day from sunrise to sunset.

Alex: Why do you fast?

Ahmad: We fast to have empathy with those who are less fortunate, and to understand what it's like to go without food and water for a whole day. It helps us to be grateful for the blessings we have and to become closer to Allah.

Alex: That's really amazing! So, what happens when Ramadan ends?

Ahmad: That's when we celebrate Eid al-Fitr. It's a day of reward and celebration for all the hard work and devotion we put in during the previous month.

Alex: That sounds like a lot of fun! What do people do during Eid?

Ahmad: Well, we usually get up early and perform a special prayer at the mosque, then spend the day with our family and friends, exchanging gifts and enjoying delicious food. We also visit the elderly and give to charity in order to help those in need.

Alex: That sounds like a great way to show love and compassion to others.

Ahmad: It definitely is! Eid al-Fitr is a time to come together as a community and celebrate the blessings in our lives.
It's a reminder of the importance of unity, generosity, and gratitude.

Alex: Wow! I had no idea that Ramadan and Eid were such important celebrations! I'm so grateful that you taught me about them.

Ahmad: Of course, Alex! I'm always here to answer any questions you have and to help you learn about our cultures and traditions.

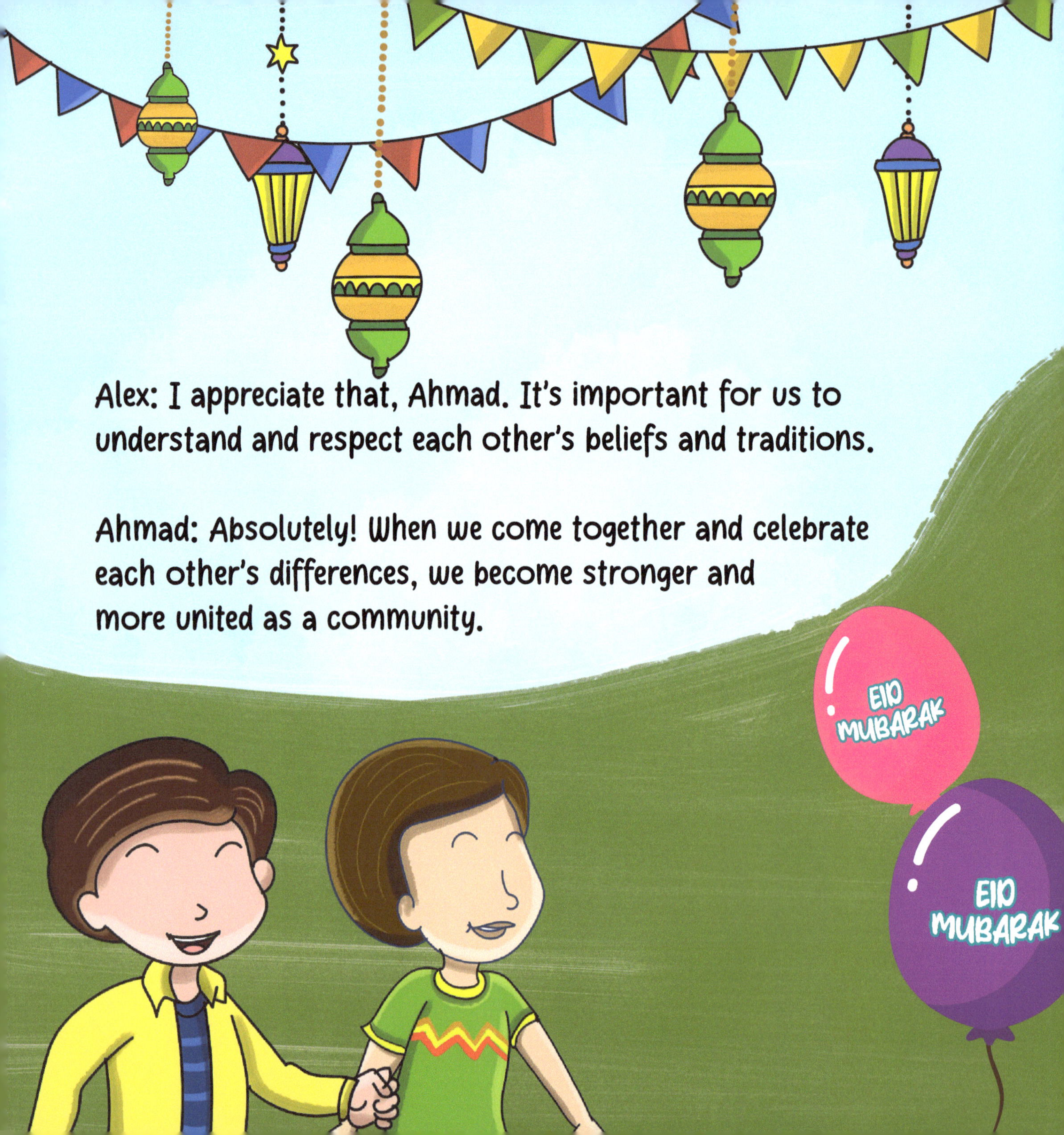

Alex: I appreciate that, Ahmad. It's important for us to understand and respect each other's beliefs and traditions.

Ahmad: Absolutely! When we come together and celebrate each other's differences, we become stronger and more united as a community.

As they walked around the festivities, Alex noticed that the children were especially excited, running around with balloons and toys.

Ahmad told him that Eid was a way of spreading the message of love and inclusiveness and a reminder that we are all connected as human beings, and that it was traditional to give gifts to children during Eid as a symbol of love and generosity.

Alex was amazed by the sense of unity and solidarity he felt as he watched the faithful coming together to pray and celebrate.

He realized that despite their different
backgrounds and beliefs, everyone was united by
their shared values and aspirations.

As the day came to an end, Alex felt grateful
for the opportunity to learn about Eid al-Fitr
and for the kindness and generosity
of his friend Ahmad and his community.

He left the celebrations with a newfound appreciation for the
importance of diversity, compassion, and community.
Alex had learned that Eid is a way of spreading the message
of love and inclusiveness, and a reminder that
all people are connected.

From that day forward, Alex made a point of celebrating Eid al-Fitr with his friend Ahmad and his family each year, and he felt proud to be a part of a community that valued love, understanding, and respect.

Alex had learned that no matter where we come from or what we believe, everyone can come together to celebrate and cherish the blessings in our lives.

Library of Congress Cataloging-in-Publication Data
ISBN: 978-1-998923-12-0

Publisher
Kids Edu Care Inc.
Children's Dedicated Learning Series
Website: www.kidseducare.ca
Illustration Copyright © 2022 by
Kids Edu Care Inc.
Canada

Illustration & Design
Bee Digital